STAR-LORD   GAMORA   ROCKET RACCOON   GROOT   DRAX   VENOM   CAPTAIN MARVEL

GUARDIANS OF THE GALAXY

ORIGINAL SIN

WRITER: **BRIAN MICHAEL BENDIS**

ISSUES #18-20

PENCILERS: **ED McGUINNESS** WITH **VALERIO SCHITI** (#20)

INKERS: **MARK FARMER** (#18-19), **MARK MORALES** (#19),

JOHN LIVESAY (#19), **ED McGUINNESS** (#19) & **VALERIO SCHITI** (#20)

COLORISTS: **JUSTIN PONSOR** (#18) & **JASON KEITH** (#19-20)

COVER ART: **ED McGUINNESS, MARK FARMER** & **JUSTIN PONSOR**

ISSUES #21-23

ARTIST: **VALERIO SCHITI** WITH **DAVID LOPEZ** (#22)   COLORIST: **JASON KEITH**

COVER ART: **VALERIO SCHITI** WITH **JUSTIN PONSOR** (#21) & **JASON KEITH** (#22)

AND **CHRISTIAN WARD** (#23)

LETTERER: **VC'S CORY PETIT**   ASSISTANT EDITOR: **XANDER JAROWEY**   EDITOR: **MIKE MARTS**

COLLECTION EDITOR: **JENNIFER GRÜNWALD**   ASSISTANT EDITOR: **SARAH BRUNSTAD**

ASSOCIATE MANAGING EDITOR: **ALEX STARBUCK**   EDITOR, SPECIAL PROJECTS: **MARK D. BEAZLEY**

SENIOR EDITOR, SPECIAL PROJECTS: **JEFF YOUNGQUIST** SVP PRINT, SALES & MARKETING: **DAVID GABRIEL**

EDITOR IN CHIEF: **AXEL ALONSO**   CHIEF CREATIVE OFFICER: **JOE QUESADA**

PUBLISHER: **DAN BUCKLEY**   EXECUTIVE PRODUCER: **ALAN FINE**

GUARDIANS OF THE GALAXY VOL. 4: ORIGINAL SIN. Contains material originally published in magazine form as GUARDIANS OF THE GALAXY #18-23. First printing 2015. ISBN# 978-0-7851-9246-6. Published by MARVEL WORLDWIDE, INC., a subsidiary of MARVEL ENTERTAINMENT, LLC. OFFICE OF PUBLICATION: 135 West 50th Street, New York, NY 10020. Copyright © 2015 MARVEL No similarity between any of the names, characters, persons, and/or institutions in this magazine with those of any living or dead person or institution is intended, and any such similarity which may exist is purely coincidental. **Printed in the U.S.A.** ALAN FINE, President, Marvel Entertainment: DAN BUCKLEY, President, TV, Publishing and Brand Management; JOE QUESADA, Chief Creative Officer; TOM BREVOORT, SVP of Publishing; DAVID BOGART, SVP of Operations & Procurement, Publishing; C.B. CEBULSKI, VP of International Development & Brand Management; DAVID GABRIEL, SVP Print, Sales & Marketing; JIM O'KEEFE, VP of Operations & Logistics; DAN CARR, Executive Director of Publishing Technology; SUSAN CRESPI, Editorial Operations Manager; ALEX MORALES, Publishing Operations Manager; STAN LEE, Chairman Emeritus. For information regarding advertising in Marvel Comics or on Marvel.com, please contact Jonathan Rheingold, VP of Custom Solutions & Ad Sales, at jrheingold@marvel.com. For Marvel subscription inquiries, please call 800-217-9158. **Manufactured between** 9/25/2015 and 11/2/2015 by R.R. DONNELLEY, INC., SALEM, VA, USA.

10 9 8 7 6 5 4 3 2 1

PREVIOUSLY...

DURING A CONFLICT WITH THANOS, PETER QUILL AND RICHARD RIDER, A.K.A. NOVA, AIMED TO STOP THE MAD TITAN ONCE AND FOR ALL BY TRAPPING HIM, ALONG WITH THEMSELVES, IN A PARASITIC PARALLEL DIMENSION KNOWN AS THE CANCERVERSE. A SUICIDE MISSION BY ALL ACCOUNTS, BUT WORTH IT TO SAVE THE GALAXY FROM THANOS. WITH THE COLLAPSE OF THE FAULT THAT CONNECTED THE CANCERVERSE, PETER AND NOVA WERE BELIEVED TRAPPED FOREVER.

AFTER MOURNING THEIR DEATHS, THE REMAINING GUARDIANS WERE RELIEVED TO DISCOVER THAT PETER — ALONG WITH THE FORMERLY DECEASED DRAX — WAS SOMEHOW ALIVE, BUT RELIEF TURNED TO HORROR WHEN THEY REALIZED THANOS HAD SURVIVED THE CANCERVERSE AS WELL. HOW THEY SURVIVED REMAINED A MYSTERY...UNTIL NOW.

MEANWHILE, PETER QUILL MAY HAVE FINALLY SETTLED DOWN FOR A RELATIONSHIP WITH THE X-MEN'S KITTY PRYDE — IF YOU CAN CALL HOLOGRAM CALLS FROM STAR SYSTEMS AWAY "DATING." AND FLASH THOMPSON, A.K.A. VENOM, HAS BEEN PLACED WITH THE GUARDIANS OF THE GALAXY AS THE AVENGERS' EARTH REPRESENTATIVE. HOWEVER, AFTER BEING KIDNAPPED AND SEPARATED FROM THE GROUP, VENOM MAY NOT BE KEEN ON INTERSTELLAR ADVENTURES. SPACE HAS DONE STRANGE THINGS TO HIS SYMBIOTE, AND AS EACH DAY PASSES IT GROWS STRONGER AND MORE DIFFICULT TO CONTROL.

18

FIRST, I HAVE SOMETHING TO CONFESS TO YOU.

I HAVE CHANGED.

AND I AM *PROUD* OF THIS FACT.

ALL THAT WE'VE BEEN THROUGH, ALL THAT WE'VE SEEN, IT WOULD BE MADNESS TO THINK THAT IT WOULDN'T CHANGE US.

IT WOULD ALMOST BE, YOU WOULD SAY... RIDICULOUS.

WE'VE TRAVELED FROM ONE END OF THE GALAXY TO THE NEXT.

WE PUT OUR LIVES IN EACH OTHER'S HANDS.

I BELIEVE IT HAS MADE ME MORE SPIRITUAL.

NOT RELIGIOUS.

MY FATHER RUINED RELIGION FOR ME.

I GREW UP WATCHING HIM WORSHIP *DEATH.*

RELIGION MEANS NOTHING.

WE'VE ALSO, YOU AND I, MET TOO MANY SO-CALLED SUPERIOR BEINGS WHO HAVE REVEALED THEMSELVES TO BE ANYTHING BUT.

AS I SAID, WE ARE... SPIRITUAL.

AND BECAUSE OF THIS, I THINK THINGS HAVE MORE MEANING THAN I USED TO.

I THINK THE GALAXY AND THE UNIVERSE ARE CONNECTED IN WAYS WE WILL NEVER FULLY UNDERSTAND...BUT JUST KNOWING THAT THEY ARE CALMS ME.

IT *LIFTS* ME.

I'M OKAY WITH NOT KNOWING EVERYTHING ABOUT THE UNIVERSE BECAUSE I KNOW I'M NOT SUPPOSED TO.

BUT THERE'S ONE THING I *DO* NEED TO KNOW.

ONE NAGGING QUESTION THAT I CANNOT LIVE WITHOUT THE ANSWER TO ANYMORE...

"A HERO'S DEATH.

"DRAX WAS DEAD-- I WANTED IT TO MEAN SOMETHING.

"STOPPING THANOS ONCE AND FOR ALL, FOR ALL TIME, WAS WORTH IT.

"SHOVING THAT COSMIC CUBE UP HIS PURPLE BUTT AS THE UNIVERSE FOLDED DOWN AROUND HIM...

"...WELL, WOULDN'T THAT MAKE EVERY DAMN THING WE'VE BEEN THROUGH *WORTH* IT?"

"AND US.

"WE THOUGHT WE WERE GOING OUT IN A BLAZE OF GLORY.

"REMIND US WE WEREN'T ALONE."

SHOOMM

GEEZ!

AND I WAS REALLY STARTING TO LIKE THIS PLACE.

MAYBE WE COULD SPLIT RENT ON AN APARTMENT HERE!

SOMETHING DOWNTOWN.

ON SECOND THOUGHT...

BACK UP--I'M GOING TO SWITCH MY ELEMENTAL GUN TO HURRICANE.

I WILL NOT BE TOUCHED!

SHOOM

TAKE DRAX AND GO!

NO!

NO!

"IT WAS--IT WAS INSTINCT.

"I DIDN'T CONSCIOUS THINK IT. I JUST--IT JU HAPPENED.

"WE WERE IN REAL TROUBLE I WAS HOLDIN THE CUBE..."

KRAKAKA KOOm

#18 75TH ANNIVERSARY VARIANT BY ALEX ROSS

FAKOOM

"STOP!

"STOP IT!"

#20 HASBRO VARIANT

THIS ALLIANCE IS A CHARADE!

I TRUSTED YOU ALL WITH MY LIFE.

I GAVE YOU MORE OF MYSELF THAN IF WE WERE BETROTHED.

AND *YOU,* DRAX.

YOU OF ALL.

I HOLD YOU UP AS A CREATURE OF HONOR.

WOW. WHAT HAPPENED?!

ROCKET, DO YOU KNOW WHAT HAPPENED TO THESE TWO IN THE CANCERVERSE?

DO YOU KNOW WHAT HAPPENED TO OUR COMPATRIOT *NOVA?*

NO.

I MEAN, I'M SURE IT WASN'T PRETTY...

YOU DON'T QUESTION?

I'M JUST HAPPY THEY'RE ALIVE.

I THOUGHT THE COOL THING ABOUT US IS WE DON'T QUESTION OR JUDGE EACH OTHER.

IF THEY GOT SOMETHING TO SAY THEY'LL SAY IT.

YOU DON'T QUESTION WHAT HAPPENED TO RICHARD RYDER?

IT DOESN'T MATTER WHAT I SAY.

SHE DOESN'T BELIEVE ME.

I TOLD HER.

AND SHE DOESN'T BELIEVE ME

YOU *TOLD* HER?!

YOU MADE A PROMISE TO NEVER SPEAK OF IT.

I PRAY WE NEVER CROSS PATHS AGAIN.

AAAARRGGHH!

"IT ALL HAPPENED SO FAST.

"AT FIRST I WASN'T SURE WHAT WAS HAPPENING.

"HE MADE A DECISION.

"NO CONVERSATION.

"HE DECIDED THAT THIS WAS THE WAY HE WAS GOING TO CHECK OUT."

I DON'T THINK I'VE EVER TOLD YOU, BUT NO B.S....I THINK I'M IN LOVE WITH GAMORA. HAVE BEEN FOR A WHILE.

I'M THE DOOR.

NO!

RICHARD!

I'M SERIOUS, GUYS...WHAT HAPPENED HERE, YOU DON'T SPEAK OF IT.

NOT TO HER. NOT TO ANYONE.

BUT ESPECIALLY NOT TO HER.

SHE'S HAD ENOUGH DISAPPOINTMENT IN HER LIFE.

JUST HELP HER FIND HAPPINESS.

I WANT TO BE REMEMBERED FOR, LET'S SAY, ANYTHING ELSE.

PROMISE ME.

RIDER!

"HE ASKED ME FOR SOMETHING BEFORE HE DIED...

"...TRYING TO SAVE OUR LIVES.

"THAT'S WHY WE LIED TO YOU.

"I LOVED HIM AND HE ASKED ME FOR ONE LAST THING.

"IT KILLED ME TO DO IT, BUT I DID IT."

AND LIKE YOU SAID--WE DON'T HAVE TO KNOW EVERYTHING.

THAT'S OKAY.

BUT WE NEED TO KNOW WE CAN TRUST EACH OTHER NO MATTER WHAT.

THAT YOU ARE RIGHT ABOUT, BUT...

...I WAS SO TORN. I BETRAY HIM OR I BETRAY YOU.

IF YOU WANT TO LEAVE, YOU CAN LEAVE.

BUT I HOPE YOU STAY.

HE ASKED US TO KEEP THIS FROM YOU BECAUSE HE LOVED YOU.

AND I DID IT BECAUSE I LOVED HIM.

AND FOR ALL THE #@$% WE DON'T KNOW, YOU NEED TO KNOW...WE ALL LOVE YOU.

WHAT IS SHE GOING TO DO?

SHE'S EITHER GONNA COME OUT HERE WITH A BATTLE-AXE AND PUT US OUT OF OUR MISERY OR...

"...OR I DON'T KNOW WHAT."

&#$%&#@ EARTHERS!

SIT DOWN! I CAN'T SEE THE HOLO.

THEY ALL GOT GRUTACKIN' DISEASES.

SIT DOWN!

YOU EVER SEE AN EARTHER UP CLOSE?!

THEY SMELL.

HEY! KREE!

YOU'RE DONE!

I'VE BEEN TO EARTH!

I USED TO POACH FROM THERE ALL THE TIME.

I THINK I GOT A KID THERE, MAYBE.

I WAS THERE, NOT A YEAR AGO, AND I SAW STUFF THAT WOULD TURN YOU--

YOU'RE CUT OFF!

GET OUT BEFORE I CALL A ROBOID TO TAKE YOU OUT OF HERE!

ALRIGHT, ALRIGHT... EARTH-LOVING FLARKNARD!

...CREDITS I DROPPED IN THAT HOLE...

EARTH.

GLARKS.

YOU'RE GOING TO TAKE ME THERE.

I-I-I-I WAS LYIN'. I WAS JUST TALKIN'.

I AIN'T E-EVER REALLY BEEN THERE.

WE'RE-- WE'RE NOT ALLOWED TO GO.

IT'S AGAINST THE GALACTIC COUNCIL STATUTES OF SPACE TRAVEL, AND I WOULD NEVER--

YOU WILL TAKE ME!

P-PLEASE.

PLEASE DON'T TERMINATE ME.

I KNOW WHAT YOU ARE...I RECOGNIZE YOUR SYMBIOTE.

PLEASE.

PLEASE SPARE ME.

AAAIIEEAAA!

KNOWHERE.
A PORT OF CALL NEAR THE END OF THE UNIVERSE.
DON'T ASK FOR THE HAPPY FROUHK.

DO YOU REMEMBER ME?

NO.

I CAME IN HERE WITH A MAN YOU KNOW AS *DRAX*.

OH, THE HUMAN.

YOU'RE THE GENIUS WHO THINKS IT'S A GOOD IDEA TO HOST A *KLYNTAR*.

I REALLY DON'T WANT YOU IN HERE, EARTHER.

SOME OF THESE WEAPONS ARE VERY DELICATE AND YOUR BIOLOGY AFFECTS THE ENVIRONMENT.

I NEED TO KNOW EVERYTHING YOU KNOW ABOUT ME.

GET OUT OF MY STORE!

I REALLY WANT TO DO THIS THE NICE WAY.

YOU SEE THESE WEAPONS?

SOME OF THEM I CAN USE *TELEPATHICALLY*.

THAT MEANS I CAN BLOW YOUR HEAD OFF JUST BY THINKING IT.

I DON'T KNOW WHAT'S WRONG WITH ME AND I NEED HELP.

THERE IS SOMETHING WRONG WITH THIS BLADE'S HOUSING--

HUMAN!

THE GUARDIANS HAVE BEEN LOOKING ALL OVER THE GALAXY FOR YOU...

CRRASH

HOW DARE YOU.

THIS WAS A TRICK.

THEY SENT ME OUT HERE SO YOU COULD RUIN ME!

A TRICK!

CROOOM

IF THERE'S ANYTHING LEFT OF YOU THOMPSON, SPEAK NOW!

I WILL KILL YOU ALL!

WH-WHAT'S HAPPENING TO ME?

NOOO!

FUMMPP

GOTCHA!

WHAT TOOK YOU SO LONG?

YOU SIGNALED US AN ENTIRE WHOLE MINUTE AGO.

I WAS IN THE BATHROOM.

OH GOD...

...OH GOD...

I-I WASN'T IN CONTROL...

YEAH, WE KINDA FIGURED THAT...

I HAVE NO IDEA WHAT IS HAPPENING TO ME!

HOW DID YOU--HOW DID YOU PULL THE SYMBIOTE OFF OF ME?

WHEN TONY STARK INVITED YOU ON OUR SHIP HE GAVE ME THIS IN CASE ANYTHING BAD HAPPENED.

I GUESS THIS IS WHAT HE MEANT...

I-I NEED TO GET BACK TO EARTH.

I CAN CONTROL IT ON EARTH.

I SHOULD HAVE NEVER COME OUT HERE.

LET'S JUST GET BACK TO OUR SHIP AND FIGURE THIS OUT.

I SHOULD HAVE NEVER COME HERE.

THE LOCAL AUTHORITIES ARE ON THEIR WAY!

I AM GROOT.

I'M...

...I'M SO SORRY...

JUST TAKE IT EASY.

POOR GUY.

HE JUST TRIED TO MURDER ME.

AT LEAST WE FOUND HIM. I WAS FEELING GUILTY ABOUT LOSING HIM.

WE SHOULD GET HIM BACK TO EARTH.

HEY, YEAH!

I CAN GO VISIT MY GIRLFRIEND.

WHY DID HIS SYMBIOTE BECOME SO ERRATIC?

MAYBE-- I DON'T KNOW.

THESE THINGS CREEP ME OUT.

I AM GROOT.

UH! HELLO?!

CAN WE FIGURE THIS OUT BACK ON THE SHIP?

THE GUARDIANS' SHIP.

WE SHOULD LAUNCH IT INTO THE REACHES OF SPACE AND BE DONE WITH IT.

WE'LL TAKE IT BACK TO EARTH. GIVE IT TO TONY STARK.

SO IT CAN UNLEASH HAVOC ON HIM?

BUT NOW IT IS BROKEN.

WE'RE BROKEN.

DO YOU THINK SOMEONE SHOULD SEND US OUT INTO THE COLD REACHES OF SPACE?

SOMETIMES.

WE SHOULD THROW THAT PARASITE OUT OF THE AIRLOCK.

AND BUY HIM SOME NEW LEGS.

IF WE THROW IT OUT THE AIRLOCK IT MIGHT FIND A WAY TO LATCH ON TO SOMETHING ELSE.

ALSO, IT'S NOT OURS. IT'S HIS.

WHEN HE WAKES UP WE'LL TALK THIS OVER AND--

HEY, GROOT-- HAND ME THE THING WITH THE THING ON TOP.

CRACCK

I'M GONNA CREATE A MORE STABLE HOLDING BIN FOR THIS BIG PILE OF GOO AND THEN WE CAN THROW IT INTO A SVARNAK'S BUTT HOLE BEFORE IT--

AM I GONNA HAVE TO WAIT FOR MY BAR MITZVAH OR ARE YOU GOING TO HAND ME THE--

I--
I--

#21 ROCKET RACCOON & GROOT VARIANT BY DUSTIN NGUYEN

PETER QUILL, THE LEGENDARY *STAR-LORD*

HIM?!

THE *PIRATE SON* OF THE MAN WE JUST OUSTED!

WE?

YOU?

WE DIDN'T DO ANYTHING.

HE DID.

HE REVEALED HIS FATHER TO BE A TWO-FACED, POWER-MAD GANGSTER.

HE DID IT.

HIM.

HE IS THE FACE OF THE COUNTERCULTURE OF THIS EMPIRE.

HE IS A FACE THEY TRUST.

YOU ARE MAD, TOGTH. AND YOU ARE SCARED.

OF WHAT?

YOU CAN'T CONTROL HIM.

WILL HE EVEN DO IT?

WILL HE EVEN TALK TO US?

WILL HE DO IT?

WHY WOULDN'T HE?

"WHAT ELSE DOES HE HAVE TO DO?"

WHAT THE HELL IS THIS NOW?

I AM VENOM!

WHAT DOES IT LOOK LIKE?!

THE GUARDIAN'S HOME SHIP.

THIS, I HAVE!

SCRREAAGCKK

I AM VENOM!

COME ON, COME ON, COME ON!

...UHHHN...

SON OF A GLARKEN!

TPWACCK

AGH! UH, HELP!

SORRY, BUDDY...

FSHAAAM

FSHAAAM FSHAAAM

FSHAAAM

YAAAGROOOOOT!

FSHAAAM! FSHAAAM FSHAAAM FSHAAAM

UH, GUYS...

GET AWAY FROM THE SYMBIOTE, ROCKET!

UH, GUYS?!

YOU ARE BLOWING HOLES IN THE SHIP!

THIS IS WHERE WE LIVE!

YEAH, I KNOW!

I ALSO LIVE IN MY SKIN, WHICH I DON'T WANT THIS THING ON!

FSHAAAM

FSHAAAM
FSHAAAM

FSHAAAM

UH-OH.

I AM GROOT?

IT'S NOT YOUR FAULT, BUDDY.

IT'S ENTIRELY ROCKET'S.

THERE IS A SYMBIOTE LOOSE ON THE SHIP.

YEAH, DRAX, WE ALL PUT THAT TOGETHER ON OUR--

THAT IS INTOLERABLE.

LISTEN, STARK GAVE ME THAT DOOHICKEY IN CASE OF, UM, SYMBIOTIC EMERGENCIES...

WHERE IS IT?

I DROPPED IT.

YOU DROPPED IT?!

YES--WHILE SAVING ALL OF US FROM CRASHING INTO AN ASTEROID, I DROPPED IT!

I AM GROOT.

OH GLARK, HE'S RIGHT!

THE HUMAN! THE OTHER HUMAN.

THE HOST DUDE.

THE GOO ISN'T IN HERE.

SO, THERE'S THAT.

THIS FLASH THOMPSON IS STILL UNCONSCIOUS?

WELL HE'S BEEN THROUGH A LOT.

COMPARED TO WHAT?

WE SHOULD EJECT HIM AND HIS PET IMMEDIATELY.

WE CAN HANDLE THIS.

ON WHAT EVIDENCE DO YOU BASE THAT OPINION?

HEY, FLASH, BUDDY... FLASH?

YOU IN THERE?

WE KIND OF HAVE A THING GOING ON...

NOTHIN'.

THAT'S NOT GOOD.

YOU KNOW MY OPINION.

I'M NOT THROWING HIM OFF THE SHIP TO DIE IN THE FAR REACHES OF SPACE.

I AM MORE THAN HAPPY TO DO IT MYSELF.

HE'S A FRIEND.

AND A FRIEND OF A FRIEND.

AND HE'S IN TROUBLE AND--

HE BROUGHT A PARASITIC SYMBIOTE ON BOARD OUR SHIP THAT IS TRYING TO ATTACH ITSELF TO US.

YOU SAY IT LIKE IT'S A BAD THING.

I DO NOT FIND YOU FUNNY.

WELL, THEN FIND THE GOO-THING.

IT'S THE ONLY SHIP WE HAVE.

SHE'S RIGHT. THIS IS MY FAULT.

I--I THOUGHT I HAD IT.

WE AGREED TO HAVE HIM JOIN US. WE ALL KNEW THE RISKS.

WE DID? I MISSED THAT MEETING.

I AM GROOT.

STOP IT, GROOT. YA DIDN'T DO NOTHIN' WRONG.

IF ANYTHING, BE MAD AT DRAX FOR PUNCHIN' A HOLE IN YA.

I KNEW HE WOULD RECOVER.

SURE YA DID.

THIS PART OF THE SHIP IS A SHAMEFUL MESS.

WELL GET CLEANIN', DESTROYER.

DESTROY THE MESS YA MADE AND WE'LL ALL--

SLUMPP

YA HEARD THAT?

AYE.

MAYBE IT'S THAT ANGELA BROAD THAT KEEPS POPPIN' IN AND OUT OF OUR LIVES.

I AM GROOT.

I KNOW. I WAS KIDDIN'.

#23 WELCOME HOME VARIANT BY SALVADOR LARROCA & ISRAEL SILVA

HA!

HA!

CHEATER.

LET ME MAKE IT UP TO YOU...

OH, REALLY?

I BELIEVE THE PHRASE IS, TO THE WINNER GO THE--

GGKKSS!

ROCKET?

YO, *ROCKET?*

WHAT HAPPENED?

WHAT *DID* THIS?

THANK GOD.

STILL BREATHING.

WHERE'S THE MEDIKIT IN THIS MESS?

WE'RE HERE.

OH MY GOD, IS--IS THIS--?

THIS IS, FOR LACK OF A BETTER TERM, THE PLANET OF MY ORIGIN. I HAVE BEEN SUMMONED HOME.

I DO NOT KNOW IF THIS IS THE END OF OUR JOURNEY TOGETHER, BUT I DO KNOW EVERYTHING THERE IS TO KNOW ABOUT YOU, EUGENE THOMPSON.

I KNOW YOUR STRENGTHS AND YOUR FLAWS, I KNOW YOUR TRIUMPHS AND YOUR FAILURES, I KNOW YOUR FEARS AND YOUR PAIN AND I HAVE GROWN TO ADMIRE EVERYTHING ABOUT YOU.

WHAT?

IS THE SYMBIOTE--ARE YOU TALKING TO ME THROUGH DRAX?

MUURF...

WAIT! WHAT IS GOING ON?

WHY ARE WE HERE? WHAT IS THIS?!

WHAT HAVE YOU DONE?!

OW!

WHAT HAVE YOU DONE TO OUR SHIP AND MY TEAM?!

WASN'T ME!

LET GO!

I HAVE KILLED FOR SO MUCH LESS.

I DIDN'T DO THIS, DRAX!

BUT THIS HAPPENED BECAUSE OF YOU. NO ONE ELSE!

LET HIM GO!

I MEAN IT!

FLASH DIDN'T DO *ANYTHING!* LEAVE HIM ALONE!

WHERE THE HELL ARE WE?

I AM GROOT.

THROW THE HALF-A-HUMAN OFF THIS SHIP AND LET'S GET THE HELL OUT OF HERE!

WHEREVER HERE IS!

THIS HUMAN HAS BETRAYED US AND HE HAS HIJACKED OUR SHIP!

NO, HE DIDN'T.

NO, I DIDN'T.

YOU KNOW NOT WHAT YOU SPEAK OF, PETER QUILL?

I'M GOING TO ASSUME THAT MEANT THAT I DON'T KNOW WHAT I'M TALKING ABOUT.

WHAT I *DO* KNOW IS THIS HUMAN CREATURE HERE, WHO WE HAVE OFFERED TO TAKE WITH US ON OUR ADVENTURES, SO THAT MAKES HIM ONE OF THE CREW, WAS *OVERWHELMED* BY ANOTHER CREATURE AND IT WAS HE/IT WHO TOOK OVER OUR SHIP AND IT WAS HE/IT WHO BROUGHT US HERE.

HEY, I'M NOT THRILLED BY ANY OF THIS.

NOBODY HERE IS THRILLED.

BUT WE'RE NOT GOING TO BEAT UP THE LITTLE GUY WITH NO LEGS BECAUSE WE FEEL BAD ABOUT OUR SITUATION.

IN THIS STORY AM *I* THE LITTLE GUY?

I'M TRYING TO STOP HIM FROM PUNCHING YOUR FACE INSIDE OUT.

HE WOULD DO THAT?

ONE PUNCH.

ONE. PUNCH.

YEAH, WELL...

...DON'T DO *THAT.*

UM, GUYS...

...AND TREE...

WOW.

WE'RE HERE, WE ARE *REALLY* HERE...

THIS IS VERY IMPORTANT TO ME!

ROCKET, WHAT'S THE ATMOSPHERE LIKE OUT THERE?

IT'S NICE. IT'S BREATHABLE. NOTHING HARMFUL.

SO GO SAY "HI"...

...BUT I DON'T THINK THEY HAVE MOUTHS.

OR EARS.

WE NEED TO GET FAR FROM HERE!

AND I THINK WE SHOULD SEE THIS THROUGH!

HAVE YOU ALL GONE MAD?!

COME ON, DRAX, WE'RE SUPPOSED TO BE PROTECTING THE GALAXY, NOT RUNNING SCARED FROM IT.

YOU'RE THE ONE WHO SAID WE'RE THIS "GUARDIANS OF THE GALAXY."

I NEVER AGREED TO ANY--

OH, PLEASE...

THINK, DRAX-- WE ARE IN THE BELLY OF THEIR BEAST.

ENGAGING PEACEFULLY IS A MORE INTELLIGENT MOVE, YES?

WHETHER OR NOT THOMPSON ENGAGES WITH THEM WE ARE NOT LEAVING UNTIL THEY WANT US TO.

I AM GROOT.

HE HAS A POINT.

GEEZ, YOU'RE HEAVY!

I WILL GO FIND OUT AND TELL YOU WHAT THE DEAL--

PSSHHAAA

DID YOU JUST OPEN THE AIRLOCK?

UH, NO...

THERE ARE MANY STORIES ABOUT
US ACROSS THE GALAXY.

SOME TRUE,
SOME FALSE...

...SOME CONCOCTED BY RENEGADE
MEMBERS OF OUR OWN SPECIES.

AND BECAUSE OF
THIS WE ARE KNOWN
BY MANY NAMES...

...WE PREFER TO BE CALLED
THE KLYNTAR.

ALLOW US TO EXPLAIN
OURSELVES USING FAMILIAR
PERSPECTIVES AND THE
VERNACULAR OF YOUR SPECIES...

WOOF!

THAT WENT RELATIVELY WELL.

SHIP NEEDS REPAIRS.

THEN REPAIRS IT SHALL HAVE.

I DO FEEL LIKE A MILLION GRUTOKS.

I KNOW. THOSE SYMBIOTES SHOULD OPEN A *SPA*.

HOW'S IT GOIN' BACK THERE?

I DON'T KNOW IF YOU MISSED THE PART WHERE I HAVE EVOLVED INTO A NEW KIND OF SUPER-POWERED *SPACE WARRIOR*.

YEAH... I CAUGHT THAT.

SO THIS MESS YOU MADE SHOULD BE CLEANED UP IN NO TIME.

YOU'RE A TRUG.

THIS IS NEWS?

YO, QUILL. COME IN, QUILL!

HEY CAPTAIN MARVEL-OUS. WHAT'S UP?

WHERE HAVE YOU BEEN?

OUT OF COMMUNICATION SHOT, I GUESS.

SORRY.

IT WAS A WHOLE THING.

WHEN WERE YOU GOING TO TELL ME?

TELL YOU *WHAT?*

DON'T BE *COY*, QUILL.

WHAT DID HE DO NOW?

MARVEL AUGMENTED REALITY (AR) ENHANCES AND CHANGES THE WAY YOU EXPERIENCE COMICS!

TO ACCESS THE FREE MARVEL AR CONTENT IN THIS BOOK*:

1. Locate the **AR** logo within the comic.
2. Go to Marvel.com/AR in your web browser.
3. Search by series title to find the corresponding AR.
4. Enjoy Marvel AR!

*All AR content that appears in this book has been archived and will be available only at Marvel.com/AR – no longer in the Marvel AR App. Content subject to change and availability.